THE
SUCCESS
ESCALATOR

DR. PETER A. FRICKE, MD; PhD

New York | Los Angeles | London | Sydney

ISBN Hardcover: 978-1-637922-71-2

ISBN Softcover: 978-1-637923-20-7

DEDICATION

I dedicate this book to my sons Lennard and Lars,
who heard about these principles on long weekend breakfasts
when they still went to school.

TABLE OF CONTENTS

ACKNOWLEDGMENTS

I would like to thank all my patients from many countries, who trusted me for more than 30 years, and who came with physical and psychological struggles, so that I could come up with a specified solution for them. The process of creating those solutions were lessons for me as well.

I thank all my mentors, trainers and coaches: T. Harv Eker, Blair Singer, Alex Mandossian, Darren Hardy, Ali Brown, Dirk-Michael Lambert, Preston Rahn, Lisa Sasevich, Andrea J. Lee, Lisa Cherney, JT Foxx, Kevin E. Frances, Dana Van Hoose, and all my peers who I masterminded with at the events and retreats.

Very special thanks go to my accountability partner Lisa from Denver, who always gave me a stretch on top of my tasks, so that I could progress much faster.

DISCLAIMER

This book is designed to provide information and motivation to our readers, and in no way should it be used as a substitute for consultation with a healthcare professional. This book is not meant to be used and shall not be used, to diagnose or treat any medical or psychological condition. For diagnosis or treatment of any medical or psychological problem, consult your own physician or qualified mental health professional, and you should seek the services of a competent professional before beginning any improvement or health program.

The content of this book is the sole expression and opinion of its author, with the understanding that the author is not engaged to render any type of medical, psychological, legal, or any other kind of professional advice. You should not consider the educational material herein to be the practice of medicine, psychotherapy or any healthcare, or to replace consultation with a physician or other medical practitioner or psychotherapist. The author is providing you with information so that you can choose, at your own risk, to act on that information.

While best efforts have been used in preparing this book, the author makes no representations, warranties or guarantees of any kind and assumes no liabilities of any kind with respect to the accuracy or completeness of the contents and specifically disclaims any implied warranties of merchantability or health or fitness or use for a particular purpose.

The author assumes no responsibility and shall not be held liable or responsible to any person or entity for any errors or omissions, or for injuries, losses, physical, medical, psychological, emotional, financial, or commercial damages, including, but not limited to, special, incidental, consequential or other damages, or alleged to have been caused, directly or indirectly, by the information or programs contained herein.

The author is not responsible for any specific needs that may require medical or psychological supervision, and is not liable for any damages or negative consequences from any treatment, action, application or preparation, to any person reading or following the information in this book.

References are provided for informational purposes only and do not constitute endorsement of any websites or other sources.

Readers should be aware that the websites listed in this book may change.

The stories, names and identities of the people in the book have been extensively disguised so that any resemblance to any person, living or dead, is coincidental. Most of the cases represent composites of many patients with similar problems. The intention is to protect patient confidentiality, while also preserving the spirit of the work.

Our views and rights are the same: You are responsible for your own choices, actions, and results.

DR. PETER A. FRICKE

INTRODUCTION

Welcome!

Maybe you are a business owner and you want to achieve more than what you have now, more profit, a better team, or maybe you just want to work less.

Or you are in a relationship and you have the feeling that it is not quite what you dreamt of, and there should be more fulfillment, love and well-being.

Or you are dissatisfied with your personal situation, which could be your health, your daily lifestyle, life rhythm, or nutrition, etc.

My name is Dr. Peter Alexander Fricke, and I welcome you to reading this book. Give yourself a high five that you took this action to have this book in your hands or as an e-book on your screen. This is a book for everyone who wants more in life than the ordinary, or what you already have. You could be an entrepreneur or a business owner, or a normal person with a family, or you could be reflecting about your own life in general. In this book I want to show you how you can get anything you want, in three steps.

This might sound too easy, but I will show you the exact way to do this.

The Medical Part

I'm a medical doctor, and throughout my business life, I have helped people out of problems and crises. I started off as a flight surgeon for jet fighter pilots who have two sorts of problems: The first problem is that they have back pain because of the g-forces their spine has to endure. And they have a lot of stress because they have to make a decision every 1.5 seconds for about 90 minutes.

As their personal doctor, I could not just prescribe painkillers for the back pain or some tranquilizers, even if herbal only, to relieve their stress, because in either case, by taking medication they would not be fit for flying. Fortunately, I had learned acupuncture, which is free of side-effects and my pilots could get back into the air without pain and stress.

Later, I founded my own holistic private medical practice. Here, I performed acupuncture, homeopathy and herbal medicine. Soon I found out that physical treatment, even with homeopathy or herbs, is not sufficient to relieve certain diseases. A lot of diseases are caused by a discomfort in the subconscious mind. Since this not only happens to ourselves but also to our family members, friends, colleagues and neighbors, we very often tolerate this imperfect state of being and accept this as 'normal' or 'age-related'.

Unconscious dissatisfaction is the underlying cause of a lot of chronic physical diseases.

The Business Part

More than 15 years ago, I got a phone call from a colleague. He said he would not survive economically the next year within the public health system.

In the German public federal health system there is a limit on the fees that doctors can charge, and there's a limit on the number of patients they are allowed to treat (this is not the case for private medical practices). Basically, their income has a federally imposed upper limit. Chronically ill patients need a lot of attention and treatment, and this is provided by many doctors without payment because their imposed budget is already exhausted.

Either they are on the brink of bankruptcy or they work 50, 60 or more hours every week to serve all their patients. A lot of this work is not being paid.

after my colleague explain his situation I developed a plan and I showed him some simple steps for improvement, so that he could continue to work in his practice, and he still does today.

Where It Comes Together

For my patients as well as for business owners, CEOs, and entrepreneurs, I've always looked for the shortcuts to success. Ever since I was a teenager, I was interested in this topic myself. I read all the success and business management books I could get hold of. I started when I was still in school. During my career in the military, and in my three private practices that I've built up from scratch, I applied these principles and refined them. On my journey, I've always looked to simplify processes to make them easy so that I could teach them to others.

For more than 25 years, I've taught the principles in medical conferences to thousands of physicians, dentists and pharmacists, as well as to thousands of patients who wanted more wealth, health, and happiness in their life.

Then I made an important discovery:

The reasons that make people sick are exactly the same ones that make businesses sick.

It is always the subconscious mind of the decision maker and action taker, be it for someone's personal life, or be it for a business.

As I had learned how to help a suffering patient re-program his dysfunctional subconscious mind so that he could get healthy again, I could now apply these exact principles to suffering businesses, their owners and CEOs. And it worked and make these businesses become profitable and thrive. This sometimes even includes a module called Success-Hypnosis for business.

These principles that can cure diseases are exactly the same ones that can cure businesses. It's what's called the mindset, consciously and unconsciously, in patients as well as for business owners, CEOs and entrepreneurs to thrive way beyond average. In this book I'm going to reveal them to you.

Let's get started.

PART 1

CHAPTER 1

THE BRAKES

The Dark Side of Life

This frowney represents everything that is wrong in your life. This can be a health issue. This can be a dysfunctional relationship with your spouse, or with your children, or with your parents, or with someone else such as your colleagues at work. This can be financial distress.

For our purpose in this book all this is represented by the frowney.

The Sunny Side of Life

On the other hand, what are people looking for? For most people, it is important to have enough money. Then, they want to have a fulfilling relationship. And they want to be healthy and happy. In the end they just want to feel good and safe.

The SUNNY SIDE of life:

$ £ €   Financial freedom

♥   Fulfilling relationships

☺   Health and happiness

The smiley stands for personal well-being and health. The heart stands for happy and fulfilling relationships, and the

Dollar Sign (or the Pound or Euro) stands for financial freedom.

The dark side as well as the Sunnyside are the outcomes, results.

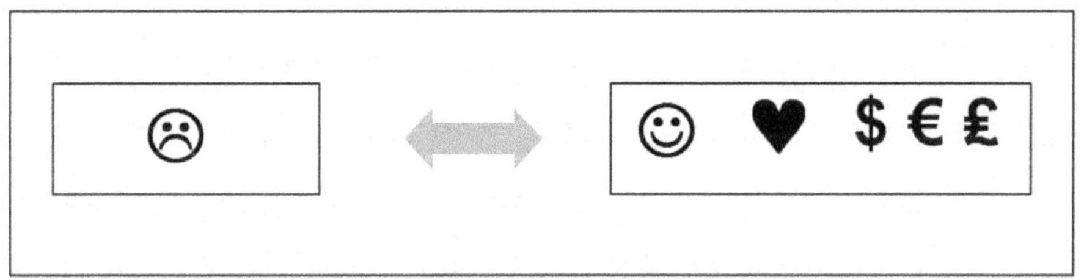

Where do results come from?

Every result is the offspring of an action. Action can mean a non-action as well, an action that you do not take. Every result, be it good or bad, is preceded by an action or non-action .

Now let's go back to your early days when you were at school. Let's imagine you earned a frowney at school, which means you have bad grades. What did they tell you to improve that? Most probably your parents and teachers told you to study more, to learn more.

The Vicious Circle

We learned very, very early that *more* equals something positive. To get out of the frowney, they told you to do more studying to get out of bad grades. More studying means more action. However, if your action took you to the frowney in the first place, now you are in a so-called vicious circle. That is, you do more of what brought you to the bad side. If you keep increasing your efforts, you'll just increase more of the frowney part, of the bad stuff that you do not want, and this is the direct path into a burnout.

Now let me ask you a question. Why didn't you just quit? Why didn't you just tell them, "No, I won't work more." Usually, they came up with answers like, "Then you'll ruin your life. This is not what we've worked for. This is not what we wanted of you." Eventually, they blame you and say, "You are ruining your future and you are guilty for that."

What just happened is that they installed the principle of

blame and guilt in your life. Everyone I know has gone through this during childhood, at school, even at the workplace and also in marriage. They have felt guilty and have blamed themselves. Remember that this is exactly what makes you unhappy and will create diseases in the end.

This book has been written to help you get out of this vicious circle, and I will show you exactly how to do this. However, it is important to understand where your situation came from and why you are dissatisfied with where you are, no matter what area of your life is affected.

The Blame and Guilt Game

Now, let's say you drove your car, you went too fast and you got a speeding ticket. You are guilty of speeding, right? A lot of people have experienced this.

How do you get rid of this guilt? You pay the fine. Paying a fine is some form of action. To get out of the blame and guilt part, you have to take an action. This very often brings you back into this vicious circle. Do you get an idea by now how this frowney side works for so many people?

But there's more to it. Who taught you this blame and guilt game? It was your parents and your teachers. Why did they do this?

They had a good purpose. They wanted to educate you. They wanted to help prepare you for your life. That was a very good intention on their part! It was nothing bad or evil. They thought that this was the best way to help you. They just did not know better.

How did they do this? They came up with goals for your life. Goals like learning to walk, learning to behave, learning to read and write in school, and getting a good education. These are the basic skills that you need to live your life. As a little baby, you did not have that in your mind. Over the first years, usually within the first four years, you are used to doing what the parents, the adults, want you to do.

And later in life? It's your teachers and your superiors, and sometimes your spouse or even your children.

To cut a long story short, they trained you to follow their goals. from the first day of your life. Remember, this was their best intention to prepare you for life because your parents loved you, and they took their life experience and defined the goals for your life. They imposed their goals upon you, but from your own perspective, these are other people's goals, or external or extrinsic goals. They did that by means of education. Psychologically spoken, it is called Pavlovian conditioning. Remember, this served a good intention for your well-being.

This is very important: All these aspects like external goals, education, conditioning, and including half of the blame and guilt principle, have been permanently stored and imprinted in your subconscious mind.

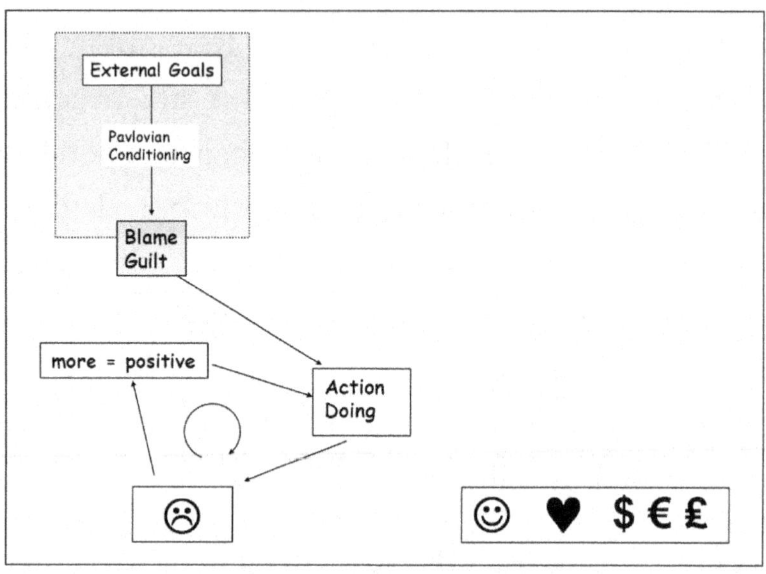

I indicate this with the grayed out area. Everything inside that area comprises is part of your subconscious mind, from the first years of your life. The nasty thing is that it served a good purpose so far, so you don't question it. Nobody does. It has helped you so far to reach where you are now.

The blame and guilt part is only partially subconscious

because we all use the word blame and guilt in our daily life, if we are in a situation that is uncomfortable. It could be that someone blames you and thinks you're guilty for his or her situation, or you blame yourself for having done something, or not having done something. Sounds familiar? Yes. Everyone is in this situation. If you see the entire picture now, this is exactly what leads you at least partially to the left side, and that is the part of the frowney, the part of dissatisfaction, disease and unhappiness.

CHAPTER 2

YOUR CH.A.O.S.

By now, you have learned why people experience dissatisfaction, disease, unhappiness, stress, and burnout in their lives. In one word, why they struggle in life. This can affect only one or all three areas of life, which are **work**, like business and finance, **relationships**, like marriage or friends and family, and the **personal life**, like your health and your well-being. You've learned that this is stored in your subconscious mind. Let me explain this with an analogy.

You probably have a computer. Most computers have one of two operating systems. This can be a Windows Operating System or the Apple Operating System. When you buy the computer, you buy the operating system that's built in. Now, on top of that, you have a choice which software you install. This can be word processing, graphics design, spreadsheets, or video editing. You are free to choose the program, but you are not free to change the underlying operating system. To change the operating system, you would need a new computer or a highly skilled specialist to do it.

What is this about? In life your hardware is your body, and your operating system is what is stored in your subconscious mind. The subconscious is the biggest part of your mind. Neuro-scientists say that the subconscious part is at least a hundred or a thousand times bigger than your conscious mind. It is way bigger than the conscious part where you create your thoughts actively. In the last chapter, I explained to you how this subconscious mind is programmed and I repeat again, this was done with the best intention of the adults looking after you when you were young.

Your subconscious mind part which has been programmed in your early life is what I call your CH.A.O.S., which stands for your **Ch**ildhood **A**utonomous **O**perating **S**ystem. Childhood means, it was programmed when you were very young and you were not yet able to express your own ideas and goals. Autonomous means, it works on autopilot. You have no access to it because it is subconscious and just like with your computer, you cannot change it on your own. You would need an expert to do that. And Operating System means, it does the same for your life as the operating system of your computer. It is the underlying basis for your thoughts, feelings, choices, decisions and actions in your life, be it the education you choose, or the partner you marry, what you eat, what you read, how much you sleep, and how much you exercise.

PART 2

CHAPTER 3

HOW TO GET TO THE SUNNY SIDE

If you were lucky, your Childhood Operating System, your CH.A.O.S. has been programmed in a way that life is easy for you. You are successful, you have a fulfilling relationship, you get along nicely with family and friends, and you are healthy and happy.

However, unfortunately, for most people, this is not the case.

In this chapter, I will teach you how to get from the dark side of life, from the frowney side, to the sunny side of life, be it in business and finances, in your relationships, or in your personal well-being.

There are 3 steps to do this. We start at the very top.

1. The first step is to replace your external goals with internal goals, which means you define your own goals for life. I'm well aware of the facts that some people in your environment might not like this. But let's go on.

Once you've defined your own goals, and now you are on your way to take action towards your desired result. But suddenly something gets in your way, stopping you. And that is the "Blame and Guilt Principle".

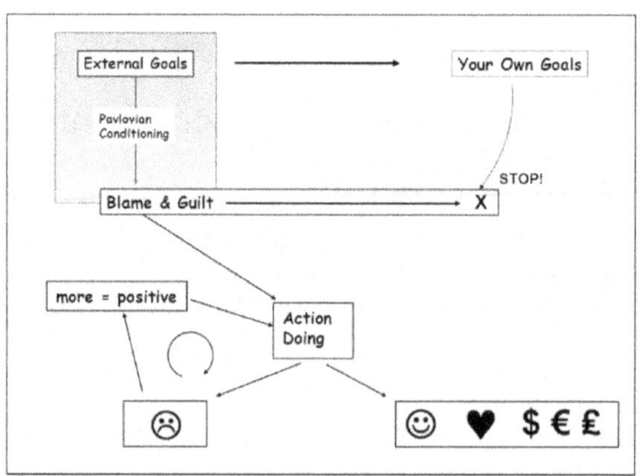

2. The second step is to eradicate blame and guilt from your life, and to take full responsibility. Yes, I mean exactly that, and in one of the next chapters I will teach you how to do this.

3. Finally, the third step is to take action. After having defined your own goals, having taken 100% responsibility for your actions and your life, now you can go to the third step which is to take action. This will yield your desired results in life and business, the right side of the picture, the sunny side.

It is important to do these steps in the right order, and we will get into detail later in this book, but for now let me repeat them.

The first step to get out of your CH.A.O.S. is to define your own goals. The second step is assumeing 100% responsibility and getting rid of the words "blame" and "guilt". The third step is taking action according to your goals and with full responsibility. As you see, this will immediately lead you to more wealth, more fulfilling relationships, and a healthier, better personal life.

CHAPTER 4

STEP 1: SET YOUR GOALS

When people are asked about what they want in life, they usually don't have a clear answer. They cannot answer or if they do, they come up with very unspecific answers such as, "I want to be happy, I want to have a better marriage, I want to earn a lot of money". However, these are not real goals. These are just intentions.

Why is it so difficult to determine what you want? This has to do with how your brain works. The brain can only process one thought at a time. Yes, this means there is no multitasking and science has proven in the recent years and decades that it is true. However, most people are easily able to articulate what's wrong in their life. This is the predominant thought that they have, either consciously or subconsciously. It can be the lack of money, a dysfunctional relationship, or stress and overload at the workplace.

Don't Just Be SMART

When you read books about goal setting, they usually deal with the business part or with finances. You might have heard about the technique of setting goals the SMART way. The SMART stands for specific, measurable, achievable, realistic or results oriented, and time-specific. However, experience shows that most of people who try this do not achieve their goals.

What's missing? This is what I will explain to you in this chapter.

While the SMART principle is not wrong, it misses some very important aspects. The first thing is that you have to write down what you want in life, and this is where the difficulty begins. Most people I've worked with come to a dead end at this very point. They just cannot define what they want. Therefore, we now go a step back and I ask you, "What's wrong in your life? What do you not like?"

I recommend that you do all these exercises by writing, not by typing, because writing brings you in better contact with your conscious and subconscious mind than typing.

Take a sheet of paper, draw a vertical line in the center, and on the left side you write, "What's wrong in my life." Most people come up with the answers for this very quickly. Now, please make a very long list about all the aspects, all the issues, that are disturbing you, that you do not like. Do not omit anything. Write down everything that comes to your mind. Now, take five minutes and do this exercise, and please come up with at least 6-10 issues or more.

Note: You can download the worksheets here: www.drfricke.de/book-worksheets.

19

What's wrong in my life?	
debts (2,000)	
boring marriage	
overweight	

Once you've written down everything that you do not like, it is now easier to define what you would like to have instead. You have freed your mind to be able to process what you really want. For example, let's say you have written down that you don't like your debts. Now, you can think how you would like your financial situation to be. What would it look like? Can you paint a picture of what the ideal financial situation would be? This is what you write down in the right column of your sheet.

21

What's wrong in my life?	How would it be perfect?
debts (2,000)	credit + 5,000
boring marriage	inspiring conversations
overweight	- 10 lbs favorite pants fitting

The same applies to, let's say, your marriage. If it has become boring, or even if you are arguing, or fighting, how would it be right? What would you like to have? Most people still find this a little difficult. If you wrote down what's wrong in your life, in the first place, it becomes easier to think about how it would be okay. Please take one issue at a time. So, if you're thinking about your financial situation, don't focus on the next issue before defining how you would like it to be. Be specific and write down the numbers. Only after that, focus on the next issue. If you cannot come up with a clear vision of how every area should be, don't worry. Just wait for a day or two and then you can fill in the blanks because your subconscious mind will have worked on this question and will come up with an answer.

The Three Areas Of Life

Do you remember that I've talked about the three areas of ? Here they are:

1. Business, income, finances.

2. Relationships, family, friends, marriage.

3. Personal life, such as health, food, exercise.

Now, take all your goals and sort them into these three areas of life. I recommend that you use the worksheet I provided.

After having defined your goals, please sort them into these three areas of life. The way I recommend doing this is that you might take index cards in different colors. For business and finance, I use the color blue, for relationships, I use the color red, and for personal issues, I use the color green. Now write down each goal on a separate index card and depending on the area of life, use the appropriate color. If you don't have index cards with you, you could also use one small sheet of paper for each goal. In the upper right corner, draw either the dollar, pound or euro sign for business and finance, a heart for relationship issues, and a smiley for your personal affairs.

You should have a list of about 15 to 20 goals. If you have fewer, that is fine too. Sort your goals according to the three areas of life. Do this now.

On one of your business or finance index cards, you might have written down that you want an amount of 5,000 dollars, pounds or euro on your account and that you are debt free. On your relationship cards, you might have written down that you want inspiration from your spouse and you want mutual understanding in discussions. For your personal index cards, you might have written down that you want to lose 10 pounds or kilos. Now, you have several colored index cards or marked sheets of paper for the three areas of life. Please sort them into these three categories. Now, consider one category, for example, the business finance category. If you have more than one goal, please determine the most important goal. Please do this for all the other areas as well.

Why is this important? Confucius said, "The one who chases two rabbits will catch none." If you try to pursue too many goals in your life, you dilute your energy and you will most likely achieve none of them. Therefore, it is important that you prioritize them.

How do you do this? You take each area of life, the index cards of the same color and sort them according to what you think is the most important one to the least important one. Since you have one index card or sheet of paper for each goal, you can sort them one behind the other so that in the end, you have a pile, a stack of your goals in this area of life, with the most important one on top. Please use a paperclip to clip this and then you can do the same with the two other areas of life, relationships, and personal life.

In the end, you should have three stacks clipped together, and each of the stacks clipped together, with the most important goal in each area of your life on top. You don't see the other goals but you know they are written down and you will not forget them. However, visually seeing the most important goal for each area of life will trigger your brain to pursue this goal first, so your energy is focused.

Other goal-setting programs, usually deal only with one area of life. As I mentioned before, if you do not recognize and acknowledge the other two areas, they will interfere with your well-intended goal-setting process and they will cut you off. If you do this for the three areas of life, your brain is happy that all areas are recognized.

You should not pursue one goal 24/7. In your business hours, focus on your most important business goal, and at home, work on the goals for your marriage, relationship, and on your goals for your personal life. For most people, this is one of the biggest insights that they get out of this program because now they see that they don't have to neglect any area of their life, but can have goals in all three of them, and see that it is feasible to achieve them.

What's Your Why?

Maybe you have set goals in your life before, but for some reasons, you ran out of energy while you were pursuing them. You lost momentum.

Most likely, this happened because you were not clear about the purpose of your goals. The purpose, the why, is the driving force, the energy behind your goals. How do you want to feel when you have achieved a goal? What is the true reason behind that? The answer is usually a feeling.

For example, if you want a lot of money or a specific amount, why do you want that? Money in itself, the notes and the coins have no real value, the only value is that they can buy you things or experiences. That is the true reason behind it. Even if you just want to save a certain amount of money, this is probably because you want to feel safe in the future.

So your next task is to write down on your worksheet, the true reason why you want to achieve this goal, why you are pursuing this goal.

Decision Making: What's most important to you

You will by now probably have a long list of goals in the three areas of life or maybe only in one or two areas of life. That's totally fine. However, if you want to pursue all the goals at the same time, you will scatter your mind's force, your energy and you will have no focus and thus, it will be much harder to achieve these goals. Therefore, you need to prioritize.

How do you do that? You take your purposes for each goal and you decide which one is the most important for you right now in this very moment. From each area of life, pick one single goal so that you end up with one, two or a maximum of three goals. Circle them on your worksheet.

A pharmacist came to me because she had got stuck. She owned a consulting company and did not make enough profit. She had joined a business coaching group where the participants were asked to run webinars. She was a mother of two young girls as well, so she thought it would be a good idea to run webinars for other mothers who are working, and teach them how to organize their day. She tried to satisfy everybody's needs, at her company and at home. This was when she got stuck and she asked me for help.

What was wrong? She had too many goals at the same time. Her business was struggling and she had to pay her employees. She wanted to be a good mother and have time for her husband and her children. She also wanted to fulfill all the tasks from this business coaching, which meant that she had to go through another learning curve doing webinars. Once we found out what her real purpose was, she could understand that teaching other working moms was not what she really wanted. She focused on growing her business and using the webinars to attract more clients.

CHAPTER 5

STEP 2: ERADICATE GUILT AND BLAME - ONCE AND FOREVER

Risks and Side Effects

Based on more than 25 years of experience, I can assure you that this part brings you to a new level of interaction with others. It will booster your self-esteem, your authenticity and your social status.

However, I'm a medical doctor, so I have to warn you about the the risks and side effects of this chapter. Once you learn how to eradicate guilt and blame in your life, you will not be the same. You will not take part in discussions with others when they talk about how someone is wrong and guilty of something, because you will have overcome this. And once you've adopted it, you cannot go back. Some people will not understand you. But that's their problem now.

If you're not prepared and ready for this, go on to the next chapter.

What's wrong with blame and guilt?

Imagine *you* are guilty for someone's situation. Does that make you feel good or bad? Most probably you will feel bad.

Now imagine *someone else* is guilty for your situation and you are blaming him or her. Does that make you feel strong or weak? Most probably you feel weak.

So you see, using the "guilt and blame" principle in your life will make you feel either bad or weak or both, most of the time. And these feelings will prevent success and happiness in your life.

How to do it

I will now perform "mental surgery" on you. That means I will cut out the words "blame" and "guilt" from your vocabulary so that you will never use them again, and that you do not accept them any more.

Just scratch everything that contains "blame" or "guilt" from your vocabulary that you use, and do not accept blame and guilt imposed upon you by others.

However, according to Aristotle "nature abhors vacuum", so you have to replace this empty space in your vocabulary with something else, and this is the word "responsibility".

What does that look like?

If you have been saying, "I'm guilty of ABC", now you say, "I'm responsible for ABC". If someone tries to blame you for something, you say, "No. I'm not to blame. I'm responsible".

This sounds easy. However, implementing it may be a little bit difficult. Why? Because you are now operating against your CH.A.O.S, your internal autopilot, which has used this blame-and-guilt game for years, and very often, it worked. So just try it, get some experience with it, and the more you do it, the more success you will have, and this shows up in the feeling of personal freedom.

My warning: do not preach, do not teach, do not explain. The more you try to explain your new point of view, your new operating system, the more others who have not learned about this will create opposition and resistance, and will try to bring you down so that they can keep being right without changing their opinion. Just do it and savour the results.

Let me give you an example. Imagine you set new business goals. You will take an online program or join a mastermind where you do some work every evening, for one to two hours, or/and you will attend life trainings on the weekends. You are very motivated to do this to create your own breakthrough, finally. And now, you come home and you tell this enthusiastically to your spouse.

What happens? Most probably, you are stopped or taken

down. You might hear something like, "If you only care about your business, then you will ruin our relationship, our marriage, our family, and you are to blame for that because you are guilty." And now, your CH.A.O.S. kicks in and says, "Yes, there is blame and guilt and I'm guilty and to be blamed." And at this very moment, you stop your enthusiasm. You cancel that new membership, the mastermind, or ask for a refund on that online course.

Or you want to improve your marriage and you come up with the idea to take two weeks off to go on a romantic trip with your spouse. What do they tell you at your workplace? "What happens to your business while you are lying on the beach, on a sunny island?" This might affect your business negatively. As soon as you think about this, you might cut down the vacation to one week, or just the weekend, or maybe only one candlelight dinner Saturday night. You restrain yourself because as soon as you pursue your own goals, most likely the blame and guilt principle will kick in.

This is pretty heavy stuff, right? Yes, it is, but I can assure you, I'm talking from more than 25 years of experience as a medical doctor having taught this to hundreds of people.

What is so good about the blame-and-guilt game?

Guilt and blame are the opposite of responsibility. If a person does not feel confident, or has fear to act, or is dissatisfied with the situation, very often this person does not want to take action within his or her own responsibility because that would require energy, thought processes, and they might expose themselves. So they look for someone who is guilty, some sort of villain or perpetrator. However, doing this immediately they make themselves a victim.

It seems to be easier to project the action part and the responsibility for a situation to someone else than to think about action steps which we can undertake on our own.

Once you see this principle, once you've understood it, you will recognize this several times every day in your environment. This can be observed in you or you might just observe it in other people.

Responsibility

You have RESPONSIBILITY where you can ACT. Where you cannot act, you don't have responsibility. Period.

Who can act for you? Nobody. Once you're an adult only you can act for yourself, in 100%. That means that **as soon as you can act** in a given situation, **you have 100% responsibility** for it and for your actions.

As you know already, action in this case comprises as well a non-action, that is, if you do not take action. That means that in a given situation you have a choice of doing something about it. Where you cannot act, there is no responsibility for you. However, a lot of people will try to impose a "responsibility" upon you where you in fact cannot do anything specific about it.

Let me give you an example. A patient of mine came to me. She was a home maker and her mother was in a nursing home.

The nurses, the caregivers, called my patient saying that her mother would not eat. My patient's brother lived far away and he called her and told her, you are responsible for mother's eating because you live nearby, which was about 20 miles away. She got stressed because she had to take care of her own family and felt the guilt to make her mother eat. I explained this principle to her and told her that she only has responsibility as far as she can act in this very moment.

Unless she's sitting right next to her mother in the nursing home and putting the spoon to her mother's lips there is no responsibility because she cannot do anything from being away. The only thing she might be able to do is call the nursery home, and talk to the caregivers, but that is the maximum responsibility she has. As soon as she understood that, even though her brother tried to make her feel guilty to get rid of his own bad feelings about his mother's situation, she could let go and see exactly where her responsibility was, and where it ended.

Responsibility means the ability to take action in this very moment and since only you can take action with your body, you have 100% responsibility for yourself in any given situation. If you have 100%, there is no responsibility left over for others. They have zero responsibility for your actions.

There's one exception to it and this is for parents with their children. Parents act for their children. They take them to the doctor, they take them to school, and they take them to bed. They act on behalf of their children and for exactly this, they assume the responsibility for their children.

Guilt, Blame and Responsibility

As you see, a big part of this world and of human interaction runs on the blame and guilt principle, because people don't want to take their responsibility for their actions. You can see this from relationships between two people up to global politics. Just observe how often one party blames the other.

If you eradicate these two words from your mind and your vocabulary, other people will not like it! Remember, as soon as you apply guilt and blame you do not take responsibility, and this applies to other people as well. If they don't want to be responsible for their life, they blame you for something. And if you do not want to take responsibility for your actions and decisions, you feel guilty.

Once you've learned how to not use the guilt and blame principle, you think and act in strong contrast to your peers. And as you fully accept your responsibility and not a bit more, they feel thrown back on their own responsibility, decisions and actions. Because you got along without this they will most probably not like it, that they cannot shift the blame and responsibility to you anymore.

Let me sum this up.

You replace the blame game and guilt with responsibility.

You have 100% responsibility for all your actions and non-actions.

You have responsibility only where you can act. You have no responsibility where you cannot act.

Now, how do we overcome this? Here we need the TCR-principle, which we will cover in detail in the next chapter.

CHAPTER 6

THE TASK-COMPETENCE-RESPONSIBILITY PRINCIPLE

You have learned already that you have 100% responsibility for yourself and no one else has. Now I want to go a little bit further into detail.

This is the **Task-Competence-Responsibility Principle (TCR)**. This is not some esoteric new age stuff, but this I learned as a Naval officer in the German Military Academy. This has been proven in very severe and serious situations. What does it mean? It means that the task you're facing, your competence, and your responsibility are the three sides of the same "coin".

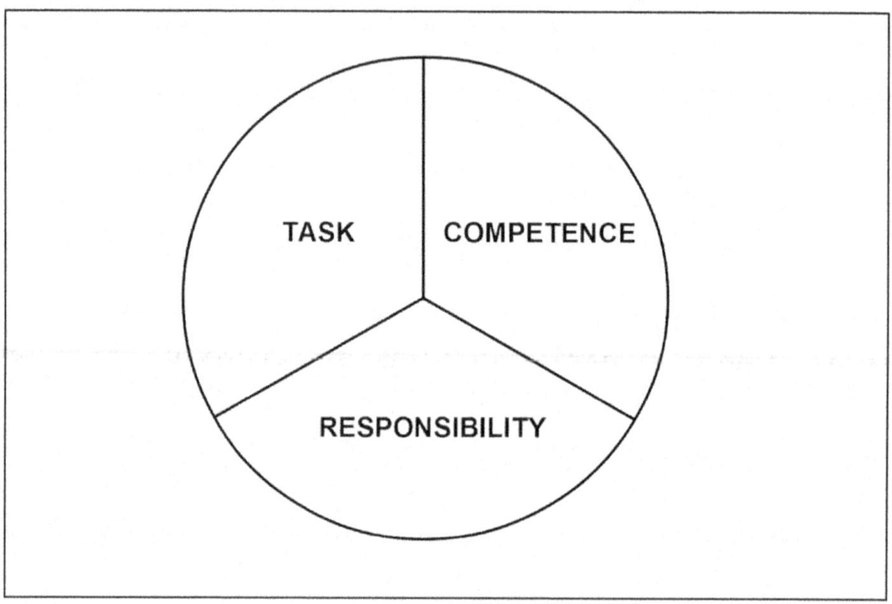

Whenever you have one part, you have the other parts as well. Now let me explain this. These three parts belong together and no one can exist without the other for a good outcome. If one part of these three is missing, you get either nothing or botch, a botch job. Let me repeat this. If only one of these three ingredients is missing, you either get nothing or botch. Let me go into detail.

Let's say you have a task, and you are competent to do this task, and you assume your responsibility which means you act upon it. Remember, responsibility means action, where you can take action. When you cannot take action, there is no responsibility. You'll soon recognize how all this fits together. You have a task, you are competent, you take appropriate action and you get a good result.

Now what happens if one of the parts is missing?

Let's say you have a staff member to whom you are assigning a task. However, this staff member is not competent for this task but he takes action, what do you get? You get a botched job, not your wanted result. You'll have to correct, to repair, which takes up time, money, and energy.

In the next example, you have someone who is competent, and who is willing to take action, but there is no task. What is the result? Nothing, zero. There is no result because there's no task.

Now let's take the third possibility, you have a task, you

are competent for this task, but you don't take action. That is, you do not assume your responsibility. What do you get? Correct, nothing!

Once you have learned this principle, you can immediately see why any result is not what you want. If it's not ideal, which part of these three ingredients is missing?

Now you can look at what went wrong. Was there a task, but you were not competent at it? Then you need training, Sign up for a course, hire a coach, get training, get education.

Or if you have a task and you are competent but you might be afraid of acting, of taking the responsibility to produce a result, then you have to learn how to overcome your fears.

Or maybe you want a result, but you don't think it's worthwhile taking on the task because you might have a limiting belief like, "I'm too old, I'm too young, this is not for me, this is too big", then you don't assume the task and you get nothing.

Do you see how this works? This principle is very, very important in your entire life, however, I've not seen many people out there who are teaching this.

If you get in a result which you do not like, look for the missing one ingredient.

And if you get a result which you do like, then all the three ingredients were in place.

With this principle life becomes much easier.

And now you are ready for ACTION.

CHAPTER 7

STEP 3: TAKE APPROPRIATE ACTION

A lot of coaches and trainers will tell you that speed of action is the most important part of success. While this is true in general, there is a caveat.

If you have not defined your own goals, you remember from the first chapter that if you are not pursuing your own goals and you take massive action, you're running in the wrong direction that is heading for the frowny for unhappiness, disease, stress, ruined relationships, bad health and burnout. Therefore, it is important to define your goals, assume your own responsibility before you take action.

As a doctor and a pilot, I do not start with an action right away. With a patient, first, I take the history, I examine the patient, and then I take my responsibility and act in terms of treatment. As a pilot, I check the aircraft first, I determine where I want to go, what my landing spot is, and what might happen underway in terms of the weather. After I've checked that, determined my goal, taken my responsibility, then and only then I take action and start the engine.

Not like other pilots, "kick the tire, light the fire", and off you go. These three steps that you've learned by now have to be done in exactly this order for you to achieve what you really want in life, no matter in what area it is. How to take appropriate action? Usually, people tell you what's the first step. I don't tell you that. We begin with the end in mind. What would be the last step? Please take one stack of your index cards, no matter which one you pick.

CHAPTER 8

NAVIGATION: DEVELOP YOUR PLAN

The last step

Most trainings program will tell you to write down the first step on your way to your goal. Here we do it differently. We start with the end in mind, we reverse engineer. This is much more powerful to engage your brain, your mind to help you on your way. Now take one goal from your list. That is the number one goal from one of your areas of life. It does not matter which area of life that is.

Remember the purpose of this goal. Now please imagine

that you have reached it. What was the last step before it was accomplished? For example, if you want to go on a vacation, the last step would be to get on the airplane for your destination. If it's a financial goal, the last step would be you print out your bank statement with the amount you desired and you file it away.

Why do we do this in this order? It is important to come up with a clear vision, a clear image of the completion of your goal for your mind.

Now do this with the other most important goals from the other areas of life.

Write down what the last steps are, so that in the end you have a maximum of three last steps.

Your resources

Until today, you have achieved a lot in your life. However, most people do not acknowledge that. You are full of resources and experiences. This is like a bank account where you can draw from.

For each of your goals, please write down what you have or what you know already in order to pursue and achieve this goal. Make a long list and come up with at least 20 items.

Now look at your goal and look at your resources, what do you think you still need?

Make another list. This can be a skill, or a specific knowledge, or it can be a certain amount of money. Maybe you need specific people to help you.

Write down that list on the worksheet that I provided here.

Investment: Time, energy, money (Budgets)

For everything you get you have to pay a price. This can be a price of money that you have to pay, but usually it is also a certain amount of time that you have to invest and your energy to keep up the momentum in pursuing your goal.

So, for each of your three goals, please write down how much time you have to invest, and break that down in months, days and daily hours. Then write down the financial budget you need.

In terms of energy, you have to be aware that pursuing something new will cost you mental energy. So, you have to make sure that you get a good compensation in terms of rest, sleep and exercise to keep your body working properly.

Your very first step

After you've done this general planning of your goal, the purpose and feeling you want to achieve, your resources and your requirements as well as your investments, now determine, what would be the very first step.

Here is the good news. You have done the first steps already by doing these exercises!

You have started already with your general plan for every important goal, what you have, what you need, and what you will invest. Now please determine, what would be the first action step for its realization. In our example of the vacation, the very first step could be to go to a travel office Monday afternoon and ask for three suggestions where to go. This first step is not a big one, it is just to get you into motion to do something into the direction of your goal. It actually has to be a very small step, not challenging, so that it is easy for you to do that.

In one of my workshops, a physician said that she needed to go on vacation after all these months of hard work. We had already determined her last step, which was getting on the plane.

But now she was struggling to find out the first step. I asked her at that workshop, "What would be the first step to do in order to go on a vacation?" She said, "I could search on the internet, or I could go to a travel office." And then she said, "There's actually a travel office at the corner of my house!" So, I asked her again, "What would be the very first step?" And together we found out that the very first step would be to go to that travel office Monday evening at 6:00 PM to get three offers for a two-week vacation.

Looking at your three index cards stacks, you read on the top your most important goal in this area of life. Now please think what would be the last step? Let's say you want to go on vacation, then the last step would be to drive to the airport, or if you want to be debt free and have a certain amount of money in your bank account, the last step would be to take your bank statement and file it away, reading that positive number. Or in relationships, such as marriage, you hug your spouse and you both feel emotionally on the same page. These are examples of the last steps.

Please take your goal and write down the last step for this. Please do that now. After you've done this, think about what would lead to the situation where you could take the last step? For example, for going on a vacation, you would have to book the flight. Please write down this intermediate step and continue writing down the steps that lead to the one that you've written down before. You reverse engineer your goal achieving process, cutting it down into very, very small, little action items. Each action item needs only one decision.

If you have more decisions to make on one of these steps,

then you have to cut them down further into even smaller sub steps so that each of the sub steps needs only one single decision. In the example of our vacation trip, you have to decide at some point where you want to go. You might go to the mountains, you might go to the beach, you might stay in your own country or you might go abroad, or you might even go on a cruise. These are many decision processes. Therefore, you have to break them down.

Do you want to go to the mountains or to the beach? First, decide on that. Do you want to leave your country or do you want to stay at home? Once you've determined that, where you want to go, how long you want to go, when you want to go, then write down how you got all the options for these decisions. Most probably, you have searched the internet or you went to some travel agency to get some offers on what's available.

The step before that would be to pick a date and a time where you would enter a local travel agency, or you sit down, switch on your computer and browse the vacation sites. Staying with this example, the step before this would be the decision to go on a vacation or not to go. This would be the very, very first step that you would have to take in order to go on a vacation. List all these steps backwards until you come to the very first one.

Now as you see the entire path clearly in front of you, you can see how easy it is to take the first step because your brain, your subconscious mind knows already where it would lead to, and that will create a massive amount of motivation to take the first step. The last thing to do is to set a date and a time in your calendar when you will take this first step, like switching on the computer or walking into the travel agency and asking for options for a vacation. Then you take the responsibility and just do it.

This now completes our picture. With the steps 1, 2, and 3 in the right order you get to the SUNNY SIDE OF LIFE.

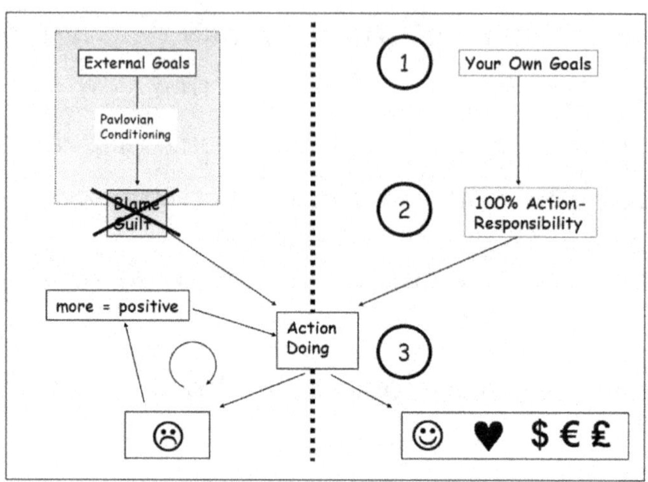
External Goals
Pavlovian Conditioning
Blame
Guilt
more = positive
Action Doing
1
Your Own Goals
2
100% Action- Responsibility
3
$ € £

CHAPTER 9

JUST DO IT: EXECUTE YOUR PLAN

Your plan becomes detailed

In the last chapter you developed your general plan for achieving your goal, like a map. Now, you will outline and determine each and every little step of that path.

You already know your first step, this is where it starts. Now, take your list of resources and needs and develop a step by step, baby step plan that will lead to your goal. What is the second step? Which third step will follow?

This can become a very long list, and that is good. The longer the list, the more detailed your steps probably are. The more detailed they are, the smaller they are and the easier they are to take. This part will probably require most of your time. Determine when you will do this, set aside a time block and work on it until this plan is finished.

In our example her very first baby step would be to walk into the travel office. Easy, right?

Then she would say, "I'd like to get 3 offers for a 2-week vacation, starting in around 6 to 8 weeks". Possible, right?

The next step would be to study the 3 options and make a decision. Now, for some people this decision-making step is a little bit challenging, because they suffer from FOMO, which is Fear Of Missing Out.

A decision always cuts away some of the good possibilities in life, and this can be a little bit scary. Some years ago I designed an entire one-day workshop on decision-making which enables the participants to make any decision of any size within 22 minutes – and be sure that this decision was right. As this would go beyond the scope of this book, I give you here a shortcut for decision-making: go for your best gut feeling, follow your emotions.

And the last step for that day would be to call or mail the travel office and book that vacation.

Now do this for the first interim goal. You don't have to do it and you should not do it for the entire path, because underway there will be changes to your general plan so you will have to adjust those steps anyway. At this point, just name the first steps which will give you a clear detailed path to your first accomplishment on your way to your big goal.

Timetables: The clock is ticking

Take the first action items and put them into a 90-day plan. This is important because you probably have to do other things in your life as well. These other things might distract you from progressing. If you have a 90-day plan, this can keep you on track. Maybe you have only two or three days per week to work on your goals so you will get an overview of how long it will take.

For every day, develop daily habits, as I mentioned in the chapter above. Use the same time every day to work on your goal. Most successful people say that they do it in the early morning hours, some start as early as 4:00 AM. I myself am a night owl so I have a hard time getting up early, but if you are able to get up one hour earlier than usual, and you use this hour to work on your plan and your goal, you will get into a habit that will bring you towards the achievement on the fastest path.

Useful tools, navigational equipment

The Checkoff Calendar

There are some tools I provided for you to make your path easy. One of these tools is the Checkoff Calendar.

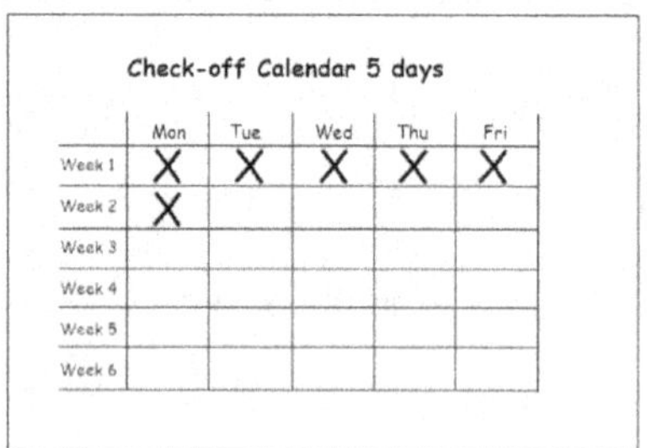

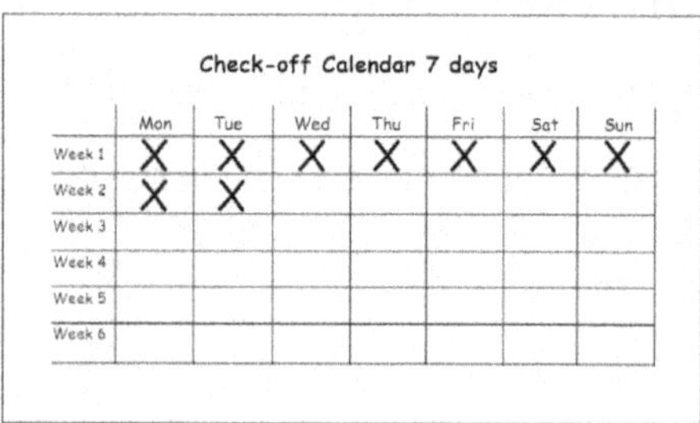

Here you write down each action item that you have to do every day. Basically it is just a simple calendar with one square for each day and if you have done that daily task, you cross that out with a big red X. Within a few days you will have a chain of Xes and now, don't break that chain. If you are able to work only on certain weekdays, draw your own special calendar which contains/comprises only these work days such as Tuesday, Wednesday, Thursday. So you have your own trimmed calendar which has only three days per week. By doing this you avoid the days on which you cannot work on your plan and thus, you avoid the blank spaces. Don't break that chain.

Business Bingo

Another tool is the Business Bingo. With your plan you will have a lot of action items. Not all of them have to be in a specific order, one after the other. To make it a little bit more fun you can use a bingo.

Business Bingo Tasks 1-25

Task 1 in the center,
the others randomly distributed

Task 3	Task 17	Task 12	Task 15	Task 2
Task 19	Task 14	Task 5	Task 23	Task 9
Task 10	Task 16	<u>Task 1</u>	Task 20	Task 11
Task 22	Task 7	Task 25	Task 4	Task 24
Task 6	Task 21	Task 13	Task 8	Task 18

Draw a box with little squares like the ones on the worksheet. If you have 9, 16 or 25 action items, draw a four by four square diagram, if they are more, do it five by five. I provided both samples as worksheets. Here in the squares, you enter all your little tasks that you have to do. Then you can decide which one you will tackle and accomplish next. After you've completed a task, cross it

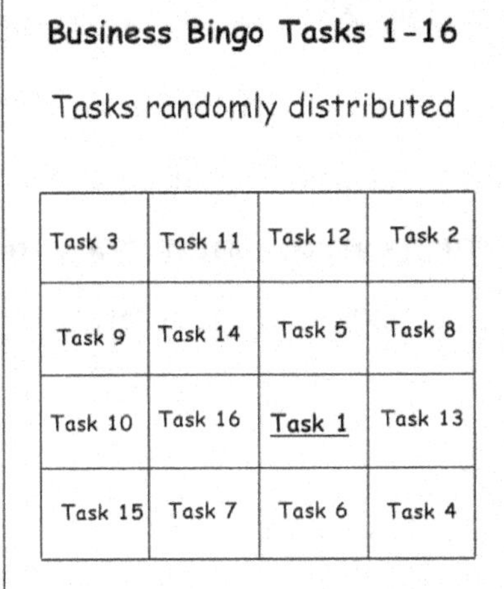

Task 3	Task 11	Task 12	Task 2
Task 9	Task 14	Task 5	Task 8
Task 10	Task 16	Task 1	Task 13
Task 15	Task 7	Task 6	Task 4

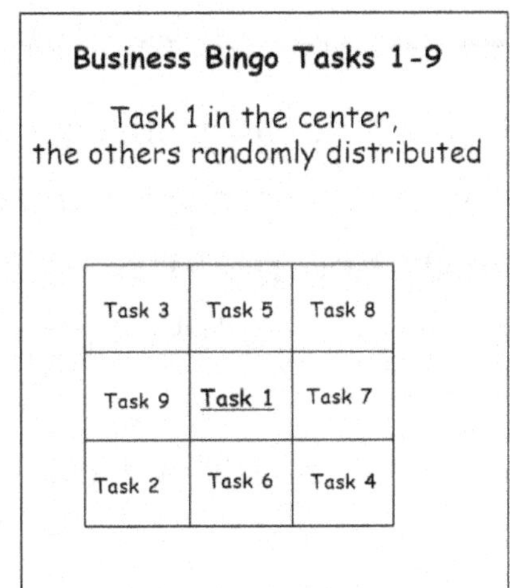

Task 3	Task 5	Task 8
Task 9	Task 1	Task 7
Task 2	Task 6	Task 4

out. By doing this you will see your progress and you are not bound to a "one-step-after-the-other" schedule, but you can choose from the open tasks the one that you will like to do first.

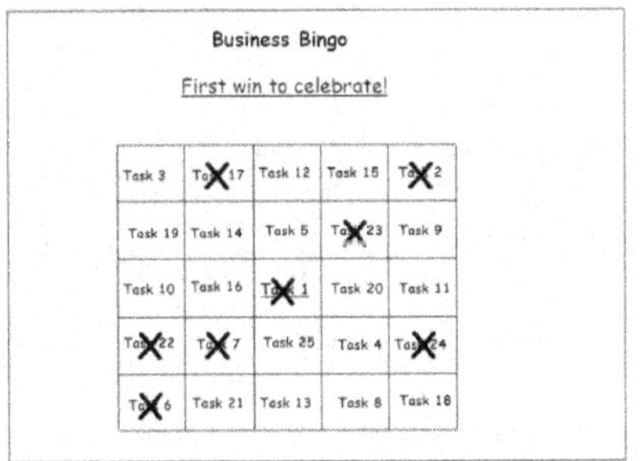

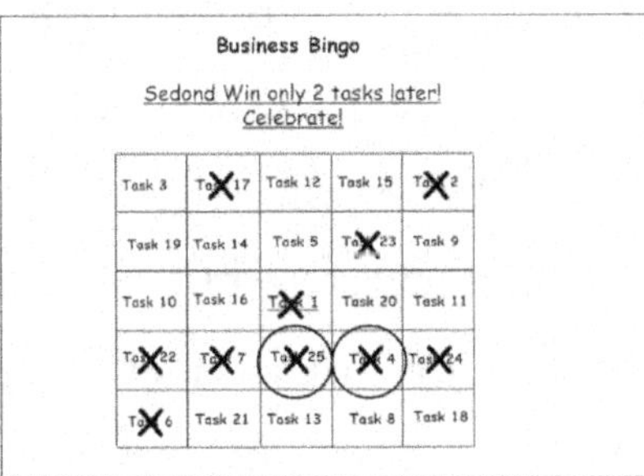

Accountability partner

If you give yourself an order, you are entitled to adjust, prolong or even revoke this order. That is a big problem! Usually, people start off very motivated, then they lose momentum and there is no one to drive them along. Self-motivation is very, very difficult in the long run and unless you have established the habit patterns and daily routines already, you will most likely lose momentum.

For this, you need an accountability partner. That is, a person who you respect and who will check if you have accomplished your tasks within the given time frame. If you have not completed your tasks , you will lose face, and that is very embarrassing.

Let me give you an example. Some years ago I attended an online course in cold calling. That is, you pick a random number from the yellow pages, call them and you try to sell your services. Huge resistance. However, my mentor Blaire Singer knew how to get us the results. Every week we had to show our results on a spreadsheet. One of the tasks was to call a certain number of companies.

Just to call them, not necessarily make any sale. This was to overcome the fear of cold calling. The resistance in me built up, but since I knew I had to present my numbers in the evening on that call and everyone in the group would see them, I found myself doing the last calls necessary in the afternoon right before. The result? I overcame the resistance and by doing this, I got a contract which covered much more than the cost of this cold calling online course.

Today, I have an accountability partner and we talk every two weeks for half an hour. I tell her what I have achieved and she tells me what she has achieved and we're mutually pushing our limits and giving us stretches. This made me achieve way more than I would have been able to do without her.

What can you do? There are online resources for accountability partners, Facebook groups. Choose a not-so-close friend who is benevolent to you, and with whom you would lose face if you did not fulfill your tasks. You can do this mutually and I recommend you do it on a weekly or bi-weekly basis. The call itself must be kept short, there is no small talk involved. It's only what your task was, what you achieved, what your task is for next week, and maybe a stretch on top of that. Celebrate each step, each milestone, and each chapter.

Now, there's the fun part. You are stretching and straining yourself mentally and maybe physically on your path to achieving your goal. You probably sacrifice one or more hours of your morning sleep. You may have a hard time implementing these habit patterns over weeks. If you only do this, eventually your subconscious mind will stall you.

To prevent this, and to motivate your subconscious mind even more, you have to celebrate everything. What does that comprise? You celebrate everything, which means you celebrate every action step. This can be done by crossing out this step on your action or to do list. Get a glass of water or herbal tea during a break. Take a five or seven-minute nap. Then celebrate each major sub-goal or milestone. Take a walk, go to the movies, do something joyful with your family. The important thing is that you consider and attribute this as a celebration for yourself. It will feed and satisfy your reward center in your brain, which is also craving for attention and food.

And there's one more thing. Celebrate your failures as well. Yes, celebrate your failures. Why? If you celebrate your failure, then failure is not a bad thing anymore. Each mistake or failure on your way brings you another portion of experience, so you improve your skills and your knowledge and you will get better and better. However, if you analyze your mistakes and you learn from them, you are better off afterwards. So, celebrate your mistakes and failures as well.

CHAPTER 10

FINAL CONCLUSION

If you worked through this book you will now have a much clearer view on how to achieve your goals and dreams. Once you know these three steps they look simple in hindsight, right? But keep applying them until they become an automatic habit pattern!

However, when you implement these simple principles it could happen that there is still something trying to stop you. This is what we call obstacles or resistance. This is totally normal!

It's a law of physics that once you want to put a resting body into motion it answers with resistance. So if you want to put your goals into motion a.k.a. action, there will be resistance, and that is totally normal. You have to focus on the outcome and your purpose, your why.

The more successful you get the bigger your goals will become, and the more you have to upgrade your personal skills. This is a continuous process.

On your way every now and then you will feel stuck. This happens to everyone on this path, and I myself know it very well. How does that show up?

The bigger your goals become the more fears will arise. They will try to keep you where you are, within your current comfort zone.

Then limiting beliefs will try to distract you from your path, with a little internal voice telling you that some goals and dreams are just not for you, because you are not meant for it. Learn to get past these obstacles and improve your planning skills and action plans.

People in your environment might not like your growing because it shows a contrast to their standing still and they feel smaller. As your energy field expands you will "bump into others" energetically. This shows up that they might feel offended. Be prepared for this! It will happen, and when it happens to my patients and clients I always tell them that it is actually a sign for growth and progress! Upgrade your communication skills now in order not to repel those people.

As your successes and achievements become bigger you now have to make bigger decisions, in all your three areas of life. Especially as more money flows in you have to be able to manage your finances instead of being a victim to money. Unfortunately they do not teach that at school, but money management like the rich people do is a learnable skill.

Here's the good news: You are not alone!

If you get stuck reach out for help. Find someone who holds your hand while you are moving to the next level.

To help you as a reader of y book I came up with a very special solution. I offer you a

Best Next Move Call.

Every week I give one (1) away for free, so if you apply now you might be the lucky one this week.

In this session I will not sell anything. It is my gift to you for reading this book. You will discover why you are in this situation, how to change that and what exactly would be the best next step for you.

How do you apply? Go here:

http://www.drfricke.de/bookreader

and see if you qualify. If so, then apply for the call.

In that session we will
– find out what you really want
– what's stopping you
– and what's the best next move in order to overcome it.

I cannot do this for everyone, but since you have read this

book and shown real interest in this topic, I want to reward you.

Be awesome!

ABOUT THE AUTHOR

For more than 25 years in his private medical practice Dr. Peter A. Fricke, M.D., PhD, has helped thousands of people get happy, healthy and successful in life. He is a former naval flight surgeon for jet fighter pilots. Today he speaks and teaches as a lecturer at international medical conferences, for the Chamber of Physicians, and the Chamber of Pharmacists in northern Germany. For three years he was appointed an associate professor at the Ovidius University in Constanţa, Romania.

By applying the holistic principles from medicine and psychology to the business world for more than 15 years he has helped struggling businesses become successful and highly profitable.

**His intention is to make people & businesses
happy, healthy and successful.**

NOTES

74

NOTES

NOTES

76